Tuttle the Tortoise

Tuttle is the name of my very first pet and this book is about what he gets up to on his birthday.

It is the perfect little book for sharing with your children and discussing Tuttle's selection of colours as he wanders through the meadow searching for inspiration and just the right colour! Watch out for his friends the Jolly Jangles as they are keeping an eye on Tuttle to make sure he doesn't miss his big birthday party!

Marilyn Cook

www.jollyjangles.com

This book belongs to

....

Scruff

Splosh

Podge

Rainbow

Naughty

Tuttle's friends
The Jolly Jangles

Sunshine

Blossom

Angel

Flutterby

Sunset

Autumn

Breeze

Snowflake

"What can I do on my birthday?
I should give myself a treat,
Maybe snooze in this lovely sunshine?
Or have something nice to eat?"

Can you see someone watching Tuttle?

"It needs to be something special,
Something I don't do every day,
Something I will always remember,
Something to make me say YAY!"

So on Tuttle walked.....
through the meadow.....
smelling and admiring the beautiful flowers.

What lovely colours they are.....

.....and then a wonderful idea popped into his head!

How nice it would be to have my shell painted in one of those pretty colours. That could be my special birthday treat!

So what colour should I choose?

"Oh there's a lovely
buttercup,
Glowing yellow
in the sun,
I could hide amongst
the flowers,
That could be
lots of fun"

yellow

Tuttle walked a bit further along and spotted lots of bluebells.

"A field of beautiful bluebells,
Would that colour look good on me?"

blue

"Or should I stick with the yellow,
I think I will wait and see....."

On Tuttle walked until he came across
a ring of delicate white daisies.....

"Should white be the colour I pick?
It would make me look very clean"

"Or should I stay with the blue,
It's so hard to choose between!"

white

Then all of a sudden a soft scent filled the air.
Just around the corner were some pink roses
gently moving in the breeze.

"Now there's a colour that's pretty,
What better colour than pink?

But the white can be nice too,
So tell me, what do you think?"

pink

Tuttle continued on his journey, still undecided, until he found himself in a garden where everything was a gorgeous green, the grass, the trees and the shrubs.

"Green is everywhere I look,
I see it every day,

But the scent from the pink I passed,
Is still there, it's not gone away"

green

Tuttle continued his stroll through the gardens when his nose picked up another beautiful fragrance,
he knew that smell, it was lavender, and another wonderful colour too.....
purple!

"Gosh this really is hard,
To pick the right colour for me,
Now I see this pretty purple,
I need a cup of tea!"

Poor Tuttle, he didn't realise there were so many colours that he could choose from!

purple

He toddled on his way down the lane when in the distance his eye caught the graceful swaying of bright red poppies in the breeze.

Next to them were some orange marigolds. How lovely they looked together.

"Orange and Red look great,
But so do all the rest,

I think I have decided,
Which one I like the best!"

orange   red

"It has given me an idea,
I know which colour to choose,
So simple now I think of it,
Have I given you enough clues?"

So off Tuttle went to get his shell
painted for his birthday.

He was so excited as he knew he would look the brightest tortoise in the valley on his very special day!

Which colour do you think he picked?

Well.....
all of them of course!

and off he toddled, very pleased with his new colours and excited to show all of his friends at his birthday party!

Which is your favourite colour?

Red orange yellow
green blue purple

BIRTHDAY

I hope you have enjoyed reading this story as much as I enjoyed writing it. If you would like to learn more about Tuttle and the Jolly Jangles please visit our website for more information.

Marilyn Cook

About the Author

Marilyn Cook grew up on the Wirral in Cheshire and has happy memories of long sunny days playing in the park or at the beach with her four sisters and three brothers. Being one of eight children she learnt the importance of family and sharing. Being the second in line she also learnt how to help to look after her siblings and to help with their homework, to show them the importance of education but also how to have fun whilst learning.

Marilyn now lives with her husband Michael in the beautiful green valleys of South Wales where her first crocheted teddy bear was created. It was a suggestion from Steve, one of her brothers, that she make a family of teddy bears and write a children's book about them. It didn't take long for Marilyn's imagination to take off and so the adventures of her cute little teddy bears started taking shape and the Jolly Jangles were born. They have many friends too and this story introduces children to Tuttle the Tortoise on is his birthday.

Marilyn loves writing poetry as well as graphic design and has enjoyed designing all of the illustrations from the photographs Michael took of Tuttle and the Jolly Jangles. She also has an amazing daughter called Chloe who has helped her with all of the marketing of these wonderful little forest friends. It is truly a family affair.

Follow Marilyn's journey as the stories of the Jolly Jangles and their friends unfold, watch them grow with your child, enjoy each character and make them part of your own family.

Printed in Poland
by Amazon Fulfillment
Poland Sp. z o.o., Wrocław